Colouring outside the lines

Jennie Osborne

Oversteps Books

First published in 2015 by	Oversteps Books Ltd
6 Halwell House
South Pool
Nr Kingsbridge
Devon
TQ7 2RX
UK

www.overstepsbooks.com

Copyright © 2015 Jennie Osborne
ISBN 978-1-906856-58-8

All rights reserved. No part of this book may be reproduced, stored in a retrieval system, or transmitted in any form, or by any means, electronic, mechanical, photocopying, recording or otherwise, or translated into any language, without prior written permission from Oversteps Books, except by a reviewer who may quote brief passages in a review.

The right of Jennie Osborne to be identified as the author of this work has been asserted by her in accordance with the Copyright, Designs and Patents Act 1988.

Printed in Great Britain by imprint digital, Devon

*for all Litmice and Two Rivers Poets,
past and present*

Acknowledgements

Some of these poems have appeared in the following magazines and anthologies: Acumen, Agenda, Artemis, The Broadsheet, Orbis, The Rialto, 'The Book of Love and Loss' (Belgrave Press), Mslexia, Moor Poets Vol.3 and 'Poets, Painters and Printmakers' (Bulb Store Books).

First to Blink won the Kent and Sussex poetry competition 2015. *The Habits of Free Electrons* was a runner-up in the Mslexia poetry competition 2015.

Thanks to the members of Litmus and Two Rivers Poets for their part in helping these poems find their form and to Graham Burchell for his help in assembling the collection.

Contents

Exponential	1
War	2
Babble	3
Safe Places for the Bees	4
She Needed a Place	5
There is a Sealed Drawer that holds my Name	6
A Choice of Mirrors	8
Heart	9
Against Advice	10
Self-portrait in Shattered Glass	11
Under Cover	12
The Habits of Free Electrons	13
First to Blink	14
Deer	15
Homing	16
Salmon	17
Avon Dam	18
Nightwatching	19
Night Fishers	20
Waiting for the Moon to Blush	21
It's not Easy being Ocean	22
Wonwell that Morning	23
Another Country	24
Caldera	25
Wheal Betsy	26
Not Metropolis	28
A Place Between	30
Ascending	31
Porridge	32
Three Seconds	33
When they told him	34
Cross Stitch	35
Lace	36
Moore	37
Woman, Falling	38
Casualty	39

The Cheshire Cat	40
The Yellow Cow	41
Camera Angles	42
Dear Mother ...	43
The Family Way	44
Offensive	45
Departure	46
Cutting His Losses	47
Engine Trouble	48
Every Week that Summer	49
Ambush	50
Telling it Backwards	51

Exponential

It starts with a book.
Words slip off the pages, mutate
into songs and slogans,
spawn rallying-cries.
Before you know where you are
hands are throwing up barricades
youths calling themselves soldiers.
A piece of cloth is stitched into a flag.

It starts with a dream
but the dream churns and muddies,
whipped up by a blast of words
blown down the centuries. It froths
over the sea walls we thought would contain it.
There's talk of thrones, of setting up,
of pulling down.
Words like *truth* and *blood* are dusted off,
their grimy past bundled away.

It arrives at a ladder and a scaffold,
a neck and a cry.

War

There's been fall-out of sorts
since the beginning of the universe,
particles colliding. Who's to say
which comes first, sentience or hate.

It's foolish to say it started
in China. That was gunpowder.
Fire-arrows with critical mass.

They wrapped gunpowder in parchment
or sometimes just wrote the instructions
bowed down and worshipped them.
It worked even better that way.

It spreads like pandemic, works
better in a vacuum. Viral contagion.
It's quite as nasty as it sounds.

Babble

Throw open the basement stacks,
libraries of glanced at, overheard, forgotten.
Don't censor blots or crossings out,
the borrowings, don't leave behind
those words in languages not your own.
Include swearwords and curses,
jargon and doublespeak. It is
between the syllables that you begin to hear
a voice both yours and not,
maybe a redwood's, old as ice-ages,
finding in a gap between too many probabilities
an open ear, a pair of pliant lips
to speak across the babble
of self-help mantras and advertisements
in a voice calm as tsunami, quiet as thunder,
I am. I hurt.

Safe Places for the Bees

Shivers, haphazard sneezes, cramps
rack a body that's been through enough –
now there's too much melting, a fevered sky
ground that's lost its will to nourish.

We fish around with our fingertips
try to braille our way through landscapes
deformed with cracks and rockfalls;
backwards, forwards, stabbing at shadows.

It's not got this way under one night's cover –
wearing dark glasses was a matter of choice.
You save seeds, I search out safe places for the bees
cradle one on my palm, watch it flail

wish I held a blue-green, parasite-free globe
could clothe it in velvet, launch it into a clean sky.

She Needed a Place

away from loud voices
where the only sound was water
finding its way through rock.

Trees had adapted
from being undermined, uprooted,
spurted upwards from the horizontal

creating double-jointed angles
trellising themselves
in their search for sky – she needed

a place to forget the claxon-mouthed townie
lecturing on granite, derricks, bridges
to his female friends

to forget phone-calls and to-do-lists,
the badger cull, the welfare cuts
the disappearing bees

men pouring fuel into a bowl of fire
the furnace that is Syria –
all those who can't get out.

She sat on a scooped trunk
listened to a bird she couldn't put a name to,
noticed the spread of bramble, unfolding ferns

couldn't get the girl from Aleppo –
burnt face, a question in one sad eye –
out of her mind.

There is a Sealed Drawer that holds my Name
after Charles Wright

It's not in my house.
I don't hold the key to it and neither do you.
My parents denied its existence
as did my grandparents, my aunts
and my Sunday School teachers.

It's not set in a mahogany side-table
and won't glide sweetly open
when addressed with the correct arcane phrase.

> Sometimes I think
> I know where I might find it
> but am probably deceiving myself.

It's not in a shopping mall, or a computer.
There are no clues hidden
among the wording of advertisements
or insurance policies.

> Sometimes I think
> there are more important things in life
> but suspect I'm deceiving myself.

I have looked for it
in churches and classrooms,
at the end of a rocky headland
and on the high moor.

> Sometimes I think
> it does not exist
> but may be deceiving myself.

There were moments
when I thought I caught sight of it
in the keyhole of
a lover's eyes.

> I was
> deceiving myself.

If I were to find it
woven into a blackbird's nest
or between the notes of a concerto,
I wonder, would I break the seal,
pull gently towards me,
look inside

or would I turn away
telling myself I have always known it?

A Choice of Mirrors

She hankers for the one
showing the tightrope walker –
lycra limbs and sequinned leotard.

She's tempted by
the lion tamer's scarlet cape
thigh boots and whip

tries to ignore the third –
baggy white trousers
under whitewash cheeks

painted mouth that speaks for them all
the lion's breath
a fall from the trapeze.

Heart

Look at this plum, its bruised flesh
torn, fermenting in summer heat.
It might have hoped to sit on a blue
bowl painted with poppies
in an elegant house with a distant
view of the sea, to hear someone say,
What a perfect plum, stroking it
with a fingertip, while a lute plays
in the background. But instead
it's been rammed into this rucksack
along with all your junkmail,
flesh on the point of rotting,
juice seeping into the canvas.
What went wrong? I hear it ask.
Where was it I went wrong?

Against Advice

Do not swim with open wounds,
it's sensible advice I should obey
but I was never one for keeping bounds.

Sitting while others bathe I've never found
endurable for even half a day.
I want to swim, in spite of open wounds.

I try, but find I paddle round and round
scraping myself on rocks – I knew I'd pay
but I was never one for keeping bounds,

and so far, I've survived, I've not been drowned.
I've braved sharks and not ended up as prey.
I'm swimming still with open wounds.

You tell me, yes, but I have only clowned
about, not gone in deep. Not so, I say,
for I was never one for keeping bounds,

my feet have lost all contact with the ground.
I'm in the current and that's where I'll stay.
I know I shouldn't swim with open wounds
but never will be one for keeping bounds.

Self-portrait in Shattered Glass

Grown into myself
a troubled twisting
in the wind

an autumn face
that tilts towards owls
calling from the pines

saying to myself
cariad   beautiful

          and what my father would say
          is that I was a good daughter

          but that was after
          when he could no longer
          see my face

this body
like a statue
shut in a storeroom
in some museum

soon it will fall apart
for want of daylight
want of being seen

          sometimes I catch her
          without the smile
          worn down   with lines
          her mother without the bitterness

Under Cover

The skies were hurling themselves to earth
wearing the grey that's needed
to make green.

Small birds huddled on the ridge-tiles.
We made a nest of cowshed stone
used cloud as a duvet.

Rain pulled down a blind
between us and the world
of four-by-fours and mobile signals

as we lost sight of hours
mislaid whole days, experienced
a blurring of our edges

following the body's compass
to find ourselves
old enough to be children

discovering laughter in all we held
to be most serious, most fragile.

The Habits of Free Electrons

Last evening we listened to owls
asking questions of the night,
sheep in fields behind the farmhouse
complaining about rain.
A thunderstorm was moving in.

You talked about electrons
how their footsteps generate heat
how they run away from each other
flirt with protons, always moving on,
their infidelity creating light.

And as I drove back
down night-washed lanes
I thought about pairs of particles too,
their dance of mutual attraction,
never bonding, never leaving,

the domesticity of neutrons,
snuggling close in a proton embrace,
how free electrons can't settle,
travel on through the dark with no company
except rain and the vastness of space.

First to Blink

And on the rain-slick road in front of me
white-staring   staring me down
daring me down   not moving
luminous in the moment   in the car headlight
forty-mile-an-hour moment
flower-face   feather-face
saucer-starer   Blodeuwedd
taking me in
taking my lethal metal jacket in
and not moving   facing me down
claw gripping carcase
pinning me down

       till I blink   brake   swerve
       into the risk of oncoming

lifts upward like a leaf
letting go of gravity
curd of mist
of white ash
dissolving to night   to drizzle
blurring to peripheral

talons ungrasped
letting me run
leaving me smeared
furred and bloody
on the road

Deer

Flash of fox-red, white speckled flanks,
floodlit by headlights they dash in front,
force me to brake, take time, take in
three clumping close even as they sprint,
spring, find space through tight hedge stems,
put seconds between their quivering
and my roaring threat.

Safety for them is holding,
closeness of fellows, melding into clan,
shared panting heaving fear into the air,
letting it go. Me too, driving alone
through dark lanes craving arms
around me, the haven
of being held.

Homing

Sky wide above soaked fields
splattered with white backs
of feeding swans,
and beyond, on higher ground
a small flock of sheep, greyed
and solid against the birds' fluidity;
their squat shapes, outlined in silver
copied in the clouds hanging over
heavy with evening's rain

and smudging into distance
what remained of woodland
straggling the field border,
terracotta roofs pushing through
here and there, like field flowers
among the sheep and washed grass

and in one house there, whether built
in brick or stone, or in imagination,
an open door, red tiled floor,
kitchen with knotted pine table
wheelback chair, mug of tea,
an open book.

Salmon

It's too early
for salmon leaping
or too late.

I'm in the right place
thinking perhaps
no time is wrong

that I feel at home here
or anywhere
that isn't home

and as I stand in that knowledge
the salmon come, leaping.

Avon Dam

Pent up here, this weight of water,
this liquid muscle with its haul of life,
its microuniverse of microorganisms.

Held back here, this Samson strength,
this steamroller rollercoaster wave,
concealed beneath innocent rippled skin.

One crack, one hole in this horseshoe battlement
and landscape would be changed forever,
brick and tile tossed aside, lives unmade

just as a word, a keepsake found can breach
my inner flood defence, or yours, let loose
a torrent dammed for years, primed to drown all

that tries to face it down
leave a razed site, a zeroed ground.

Nightwatching
after a painting by Sarah Bee

Still moon time, moon country
a little longer, the river a spill
of mercury creased in place,
clasping banks in cold.

These pools hold reputation,
unfinished tales they're not telling.
Hearts stop soon
in their ice-blue suspension.
To walk here now
is to hold breath against discovery.

Moon and river keep gate, take toll,
mime a litany of names.
All the time, mist seeps in.
Sunrise is not a certainty;
under the ribs, the hearth needs tending.

Cup hands, breathe up the flame,
hold to wool for fingers, leather
to keep firm footing on land.

Night Fishers

They sit inside their tents all night
tracking the shift from black to grey,
the moment when the time is right,

but hours drag and space is tight;
it's more than a game they choose to play
by sitting in their tents all night

on standby, waiting for a bite
or paling sky that means another day,
perhaps a moment when the time is right;

not talking, seeing what's out of sight,
each with a demon that won't go away –
they sit inside their tents all night

and think about the many things that might
have been, if they had found a different way
in moments when the time was far from right,

and even as the sky gets light
they have no place to go, so stay.
Somehow, the time is never right.
They still sit in their tents all night.

Waiting for the Moon to Blush

We shiver on the planked verandah
as wind whips the coast into fret and panic.
Two goats, marooned the wrong side of a fence
bleat at the manic drumfire of the storm.

Slowly, from her south-west cheek, we see
a blood-red flush creep up across her disc –
not fresh-cut scarlet but brownish like
stained bandages – until her face shines
fever-fleshed between the clouds,
washes heaving trees in uneasy light.

Our hostess complains about the iniquity of taxes,
the bums who hang out on the shore road.
She is hanging on here, failing to hold it together.
I bite my tongue, she has been kind,
hunting out teabags and towels.
We're all displaced, perhaps, by storms.

Back in the cabin, I think of the hobos, pushed
to the edge in their own island. Wonder what
they make of this murky moon.

It's not Easy being Ocean

I'm ready to accept sunlight
trickling across my body
as a kiss, a token of affection
or desire on a hot summer afternoon
when I'm feeling lazy.
Raindrops are less easy – they sting
like my own words thrown back at me.

It's the sullenness of clouds
that flips my mood to grey,
churns me up. I can
almost hear Sky's excuses
about not wanting to upset
the natural order.

It's been millennia.
Cradling the land, pulled this way
and that by the whim of his sidekick
who looks pretty close to him
never mind his talk about light-years
between them. It's anything but easy.

It makes me froth at the mouth, the way
he won't let me get close.
Some bloody stretch of coast
is going to take a hammering tonight.

Wonwell that Morning

Slipway greased with salt and slime,
sea rushing in like a schoolful
of children in a race with clouds,
ready to rewrite the script
it sketched the night before in sand.

I remember how a small stream hurried
through the reeds, impatient
to join the fun, past the stink of heaped
bladderwrack, dunlin rummaging
with metal-detector beaks,

how I walked with a choice in each pocket
trying to reach an eye in the weather,
a haven to step out of my dilemma,
while all the time the tide clamoured in
demanding an answer.

Another Country
L P Hartley: 'The past is a foreign country'

I find myself on a train, slicing its way
faster than I believed possible
through tarmac-laced country,
studded with high-rise glass.

I don't know the destination
but the stations *en route*
look unpromising,
their flickering displays and plastic fascias.

The miles shrink in on me,
heading for a 24-hour terminal
where pen then voice become obsolete,
touch reserved for button, pad, screen.

I want this train to stop
at a lonely platform
in the middle of trees,
want to clamber down
from its double-glazed safety door,
take a muddy path
through oaks and beeches,
lift their leaves to my face,
rub against their rough bodies,
find the slow track
back home.

Caldera

She tries to describe the shade of moss
that hangs like lametta on the pines.

It is the colour of stillness.
Words like mint or *eau de nil*

are in another language
one that contains swimming pools and cocktails.

She doesn't know the language
for this place.

Even birds, dumb in the face of rock
scorched in its birth, avoid the mountain.

It is old enough, burnt and scarred enough
to offer its cold blessing

its smother of cloud and needle
ask for nothing.

Wheal Betsy
after a print by Anita Reynolds

This is a broken place
earth's bones hacked at, blown apart
plundered for their marrow

a place of hot and cold
of dank, of water ooze and drip
of hot fuse, hot spark, blast and blood

of broken men
of bones at angles
under granite

crimson in the skull
as lungs strain
air runs thin

nothing is written in straight lines here
history crooked
as a flawed seam

ledgers balanced
in the graveyard

cracked and scattered
gutted of gear and tackle
the place of breaking
broken open.

***

You don't see the whole picture
at first

Wheal Betsy has faces
she doesn't show

You might spot a window
high up under the roofline

holding a darkness
that doesn't belong in daylight

Come at it from another angle

notice the pitted stonework
rough under your fingers

see spaces
where metal used to hang

a suggestion of cogs and wheels
that aren't quite there

Whichever way you come at it

let the wind guide you
to the frequency

snatches of bal maidens singing
clatter of pick and pail

rough greetings   underground banter
iron scaffold creaking   grinding

Half close your eyes

Can you see the grey line trudging?
Flash of red kerchief?

Door to the underworld
banging shut?

Not Metropolis
after George Grosz's painting, 'Metropolis'

I want to bring them here
to a garden with apple trees and lavender,
these automata trapped
in Grosz's Metropolis –

this bowler hatted man
too neat in his purple suit
his skull-face grinning
eyes wild with watching his back –

I want to give him a trowel
a watering can, a sack of compost
set him free on the borders
and the raised beds –

this woman wearing little beyond
hat and garter, costume of pneumatic
female body, strutting on six-inch heels
face closed and absent –

I want to sit her on the terrace
with cup of tea and seed catalogue
and all the time in the afternoon
to herself –

this waiter striding out of picture, away
from café windows with half-furled blinds
neck bulging over his starched collar
jaw clenched –

I want to show him greenhouse and potting shed
let him trundle the wheelbarrow
round the lawn without ever having
to put stuff in, take stuff out –

and this poised city dog
cursed with collar and ribbon
tail held high in hope
of dustbins and lampposts –

I want to set him free
to dash round the garden
through the trees chasing squirrels
shaking off his bow –

to bark his *yes, yes, yes*
to passing clouds

until the woman lifts her head
from her page, the man from
his trowel, the waiter looks out
round the shed door

smile shyly at each other, say
yes, this is us, this is good.

A Place Between

Back to a place I've never been
where air is light and light is green
where shade is breath and breath is steam

where ferns and lichens showcase green
in all its moods – a place between
the worlds of fairy, story, dream

peopled with dryads, elves, a gleam
of unicorn, Jack in the Green
two children lost, a fairy queen.

Greenwoods stand outside time, have seen
glaciers' slow havoc, earth unseamed
remade by rock and root and stream

where shade is breath and breath is steam
where air is light and light is green.
Back to a place I've never been.

Ascending

It wasn't Vaughan Williams
but I heard it on the cliff path
with a man who appreciates birds

and much as I savour that moment on the CD
when a violin bursts through the clouds

it's nothing to that stretch between Lizard and Coverack
heat pounding me to liquid
sundress matching the gorse

the original singer
the original song.

Porridge

It called to me
as I came up the path
through hollyhocks and lavender,
its sweet aroma
swamping theirs.

I knocked on the blue door,
was only going to ask
for a cup of water,
but it gave a little,
didn't resist my push

and there on the table,
steam still rising,
three full bowls.
I called out. I did.
Couldn't work out
why anyone would leave it there
uneaten.

It had been days of
nothing but the last sour berries
the hunger-rat gnawing my stomach.

Three bowls.
I started with the smallest.
Creamy. Thick.
Nutmeg and a hint of cinnamon.
A jug of honey to pour.
One bowl led to another.

Tell me, could you have walked
back out into the forest,
left it to go cold?

Three Seconds

You might have worried about boredom,
how he swims round this tank all day,
same rock, same artificial coral, same green frond

might have noticed he doesn't seek variety,
no figure eights, no curious response
to fingers tapping on the glass

might wonder if his ritual patrol
spells desperation or content
or if in his eternal present

all there is, is this –
rock, weed and coral,
always there and always new;

whether this fish who's left
misses the companion you found floating
belly up last week –

but you're too busy answering
the thin voice huddled in the chair.
Where's mother?   When am I going home?
          Where's mother?

Three seconds is reputedly the memory span of a goldfish

When they told him

he said nothing for a while
let soft words wash over
fail to sink in

asked if he would like
a cup of tea, he sighed
yes please   oh dear

by the time his daughter came
words had formed
into a story he didn't yet believe

boiled eggs for tea
both settling for a nap
and she didn't wake up

at the funeral he mouthed
all the words in the book then sat
in the hotel repeating his script
thank you   it was good of you to come

for a week he sat in his room
letting silence permeate
until he realised the cloth
was lifted   the cage door open

and from his chest
up his throat and out of his mouth
a canary burst
started to sing

Cross Stitch

I'm careful to let no blood stain my stitches
when my finger slips and the stab in my palm
feels like penance.
Tears are another matter.

This is my way of remembering,
making real those babies I didn't know
so mother doesn't have to hold them alone.

Since father died
she's somewhere I can't reach, repeats
their names, Alice, John, Elizabeth ...
We are not enough, my little brother, sisters, me.

He used to call me his sweet Annie,
sit me on his knee.

All I can do – names in silk crosses
on a woollen graveyard, father last.
I want to unstitch the years,
unstitch the lines on mother's face,
the veils over her eyes,
bring them all back.

Anna Maria Smales aged 11 stitched a sampler with the names and dates of birth of her siblings, plus dates of death of 5 of them and her father.

Lace

She is a puppet master
sending her bobbins running   backwards   forwards
left to right on her lap-sized stage
dancing around shiny maypoles.

She is a virtuoso
playing her curious dulcimer
of threads and pegs
creating silent music in cotton.

She is a florist
each sprig a flower, lily, rose, snowdrop,
she sews into a garden
a Queen might wear at her wedding.

She is a survivor
while her eyes last, fingers keep up their dance
producing drifts of tamed winter
creating bread, butter, cheese for the table
making one shilling a day.

Moore

He speaks where words fall short,
lets eye describe to hand
and what we call our heart
how curve and angle,
shadow, grain or flaw
spell longing conjoined
with rejection, abhorence
with desire.

Across the room this conversation
resonates. Tension shivers
in wired frames, emptiness
seeps away through holes
and every step I take
throws into new relationship
each large reclining figure;
how these archway arms,
and these, try to protect
and fail.

Woman, Falling
after a painting by Geoff Nickolls

Look, how you unfloor me
butterslipping feet and
arms at angles
my colours stolen
flesh repainted bruise
face smeared shadow
muscles taut
waiting for saving hand
or impact.

No end to this falling.
You turn to catch me where I'm not
missing me your destiny –
mine, not to be caught.

Casualty

She stands and waits,
a waif made up as a Barbie doll,
lets twenty years' hurt puddle her eyes
thinking of chances that never came.
Patience is gouged in every line, her neck
steel cords wound round a wooden spar.
The girl she was flaps birdlike in each gesture,
then subsides.

A door slams – and her flinch
is one in a long line of nervous shies
caught in a hall of mirrors, years
of shouts and slamming doors. Your eyes
flick to the purple at her wrist.
You understand the pancake layer,
panda sockets, wish
you had a wand.

Tell me, you say.

The Cheshire Cat

has the right of it.
This pine branch scratches
and he itches for
his saggy red armchair.

He knows
what is wanted of him.

Yellow teeth, stinking breath,
claws stained with his last meal
and manky ginger fur
are not desirable

so he makes a graceful exit
leaves his admirers
with what they came for,

all-knowing, all-accepting,
his smile.

The Yellow Cow
after the painting by Franz Marc

She kicks up her heels
in a landscape escaped
from the ordinary. Nothing
in this world the painter
opens a window to
is dull. Beyond our spectrum
she is a sunflower in marigold fields
among hills that twist,
cavort away from form
into horns and tails, ready
to leave their groundedness, leap
into animation.

Her sisters graze the orange pasture,
blend in, pretend not to notice.
She is kicking up her heels
eyes closed in ecstasy, pushing
the trees aside, re-making
her universe, dreaming
into existence a new way
of being cow.

Camera Angles

Take this boat, picked up
from its English beach,
cut and pasted onto a Hawaiian shore –
only those in the know would recognise
the name painted on its side in black and white
Oystercatchers Café – no Pacific seafood shack
but a Devon restaurant, offering
comfort of pasties, tea and scones.

And when, or if, we look back at the shots
you took on what will be
my only visit to that island half a world away,
the cracks won't show, the smiles
will have been pasted in from somewhere else,
a wide-lensed story about holiday fun,
garlands and happy families

just as the snaps my father took
back before digital or photoshop
show a domestic scene – my mother
and me inside a caravan, with aprons
over sundresses and rictus smiles,
baguettes in each left hand, pointing
at an enormous cheese, the knives
grasped in our right hands barely seen.

Dear Mother ...

... I'm sending back
all the words you tried to pack for my lifetime.
I never took to smart or fringe,
to nice or neat or frilly.

I hope you're not too disappointed I've
found some that suit me better –
scarlet, vermilion, flare, cascade,
not to mention jazz and jive.

I didn't find that badge fitted me
any better than pigeon-hole.
Dressing-gown on the other hand
goes very well with lounge.

So I'm stepping out from your dictionary,
with prance, tarantella, firework.
I've no room for porridge, ladylike, vest –
I'm gorgeous, I'm glory, I'm glowing.

Next time you visit, I'll offer you
tangerine, harlequin, vanilla,
see if you can
learn smile.

The Family Way

What is nobody telling me?

About all the babies swept under the beds.

Where do the babies come from?

*From adults who can't keep within the outline
who spill their colours over the page.*

What happens to the babies?

*They grow up with an extra shadow
that everyone pretends they can't see.*

Have I got an extra shadow?

No, but your brother had.

Why can't grown-ups keep inside the lines?

You'll know when you're a grown-up.

When can I be a grown-up?

When you've learnt how to use your colours.

Do I have to stay inside the lines?

*That's up to you. But this family
believes in boundaries.*

Like a tall privet hedge?

If privet had thorns.

What happens if I wander outside the hedge?

*You are not one of the family.
You will be swept under the bed.*

Offensive

We'd taken the easy option, scaling
Table Mountain by cable car, jostled
by Germans, Yanks, a couple of Brits.
Teeshirts with Mandela's face, the new
rainbow flag on their rucksacks.

Sun was on the offensive.
I was ready for tea and cakes
in the colonial left-over that served
as a café. We picked a window seat
with the view we'd come for.

The waitresses were blonde and strident,
décor Afrikaaner kitsch. We told
ourselves they were busy, we had time,
watched the changing colours of the sky.
Brits, Swedes, Dutch all came and went.

Still thirsty, I looked round for service
but none of the blondes would catch my eye.
You got up, hefted your canvas bag
onto a shoulder tanned mahogany, ran
fingers through curly black hair. *Let's go.*

Departure

We'd made the bus station by half past six
to find the café closed
although the coach was standing.
Plymouth sidled around us
a seedy character in a stained raincoat.
Dawn wasn't sure it could be bothered
considering the drizzle, but I was glad
not to see clearly the flaking paintwork
or his expression.

He put down his bags
by the steel railing, flexed his shoulders.
I feel lighter, he said, *already*
and I saw grey drain from his face
as he turned, a first tentative finger of light
stroking the corrugated roof.
I thought of the drive home, stopping
for breakfast or coffee, taking my time,
the road brightening ahead.

Cutting His Losses

First, he selects a sheet of glass,
ruby, hardest to work, most saleable,
or fickle amber, whose colour may strike
to lemon or flame in the kiln.

He cuts it to size, trimming the excess,
sweeps thin strips into the bin.

He savours the silence, no cut-across comments,
no telephone summons, no bosses,
no papers that no-one reads.

Deep red today. He picks a mould,
handcarved, his own design,
positions the thin sheet,
opens the kiln door, slips it in
to cook, to slump.

Now, the measured alchemy,
watching the dial, boosting, slowing,
allowing it time to anneal,
knowing a moment's distraction could mean
a heap of blood-red waste.

He takes last night's cooled bowl,
one of the tricky amber batch,
runs his knife around the rim
following the course mapped out in his mind,
spurs that don't fit his pattern
cut away.

Upstairs, the cabinets of files,
the last job, and the one before,
papers never published,
programmes not adopted.
Tomorrow, he thinks, a bonfire.

He holds the bowl to the light.
One more run through the kiln
to soften sharp edges.
One more chance of it cracking, ending in pieces.
Sweeping out, starting again.

Engine Trouble

Blue diesel fumes, rattles and slaps,
engine choking like a stifled curse.
Close your front door. Fasten the window catch.
Turn on CD player, radio – search
for dance music, something with rap.

Look up, focus on rows of birds on red-tiled roofs.
Ignore his splattered car in your front drive
spewing bile. It will be over soon.
Now's not the time
to offer tea or one more jibe

or even tears. Turn up the knob.
Put on the kettle. Sing along.
Tell yourself it's plumbing
or a heavy bass you hear.
Not the knocker, not the slam of a car door.

Every Week that Summer

I drove across the moor
to cry on its far side.

Once I stopped in a valley of ponies
with a bleached tree
whose branches reached for sky.

Somehow I had crossed a stream,
couldn't get back.
I on my two legs was singular.
The ponies sidled their togetherness.

Under my feet was marsh.
I failed to reach the ponies, to see
how they had made it to the other side.
They looked at me down their long faces,
turned away.

It was a tired trek round,
a scramble of rock, scree and gorse.
Footing failed in unexpected places.

When I reached the road
I was not where I had started
or thought I might come up –
feet and legs marked with a stain
that will not wash out.

Ambush

It has to be November
and I'm ambushed
by Mendelssohn
the violin concerto
old favourite
I skip over these days.

I'm clutching the pine table
find myself staring
at rain pouring from a choked gutter
an old cloth
abandoned in the yard
grey as the day.

I want to rescue it
wring out dirty water
wring out Mendelssohn's notes
and pain in some deep part I can't name,

change the music to Pachelbel or Bach
something that believes
in a pattern,
get back to clean and white again.

Telling it Backwards

Before nothing
there was a bed, low voices,
a hand on my pulse,
faces bending towards me,
unfocused like a net of fishscales
until they blinked to clarity.
Dozing, waking, each time
a little more life in my body.
Syringes that pumped in blood,
sucked out clear fluid.

Nurses in pink overalls
went and came,
lifted my head to drink,
retreated smiling, carrying a beaker.
They seemed to think I knew them.
Knowing was too much effort.

An old man backed through the door,
turned towards me, fussing with a stick.
The girl held his arm as he leant forward,
his face a crumpled mask
that had outlived its usefulness,
tears wetting its grey valleys.
I knew, not who he was, but that
I'd always known him.

Goodbye, my darling, he said.

Oversteps Books Ltd

The Oversteps list includes books by the following poets:

David Grubb, Giles Goodland, Alex Smith, Will Daunt, Patricia Bishop, Christopher Cook, Jan Farquarson, Charles Hadfield, Mandy Pannett, Doris Hulme, James Cole, Helen Kitson, Bill Headdon, Avril Bruton, Marianne Larsen, Anne Lewis-Smith, Mary Maher, Genista Lewes, Miriam Darlington, Anne Born, Glen Phillips, Rebecca Gethin, W H Petty, Melanie Penycate, Andrew Nightingale, Caroline Carver, John Stuart, Rose Cook, Jenny Hope, Hilary Elfick, Jennie Osborne, Anne Stewart, Oz Hardwick, Angela Stoner, Terry Gifford, Michael Swan, Maggie Butt, Anthony Watts, Joan McGavin, Robert Stein, Graham High, Ross Cogan, Ann Kelley, A C Clarke, Diane Tang, Susan Taylor, R V Bailey, John Daniel, Alwyn Marriage, Simon Williams, Kathleen Kummer, Jean Atkin, Charles Bennett, Elisabeth Rowe, Marie Marshall, Ken Head, Robert Cole, Cora Greenhill, John Torrance, Michael Bayley, Christopher North, Simon Richey, Lynn Roberts, Sue Davies, Mark Totterdell, Michael Thomas, Ann Segrave, Helen Overell, Rose Flint, Denise Bennett, James Turner, Sue Boyle and Jane Spiro.

For details of all these books, information about Oversteps and up-to-date news, please look at our website and blog:

www.overstepsbooks.com
http://overstepsbooks.wordpress.com